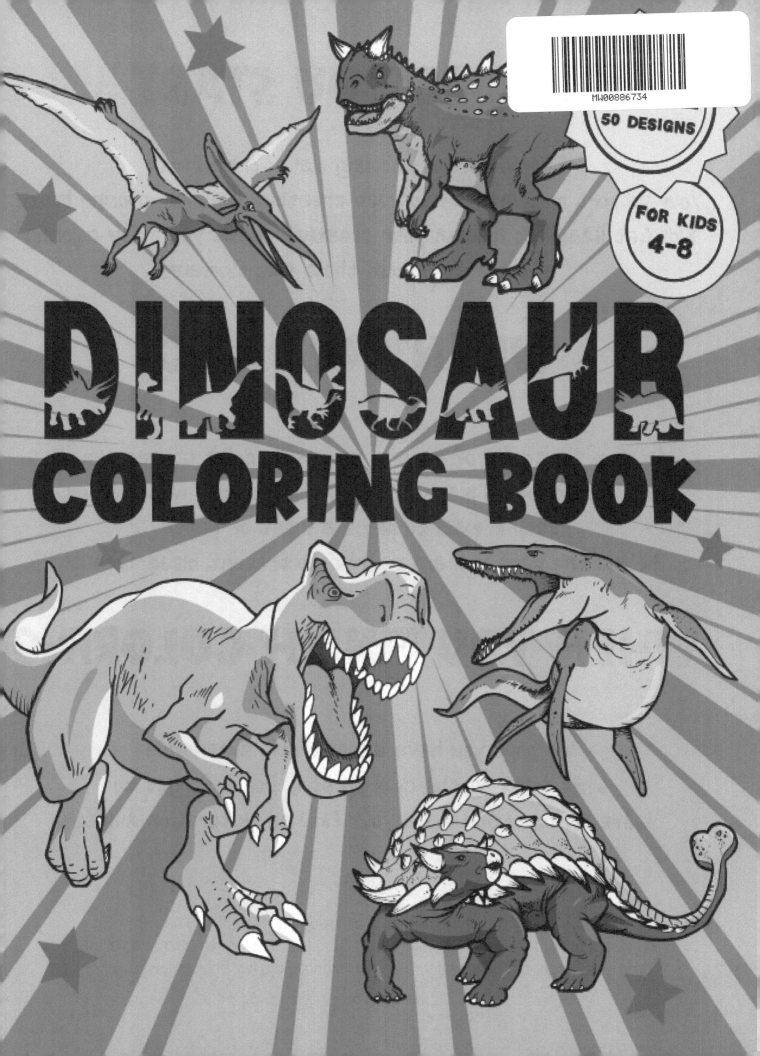

BEFORE YOU START

Thank you for choosing our coloring book.
Your support motivates us to keep creating awesome coloring books.
Kids Get Ready to unleash your creativity while you enjoy coloring
and learning about these epic dinosaurs.

WHEN COLORING

Amazon's selection of paper is most suited for colored pencils
and alcohol-based markers. When coloring with wet medium,
keep in mind to place a sheet of paper
behind the page you are coloring to prevent bleed-through.

WHEN YOU FINISH COLORING

We hope you have a memorable experience
while exploring this coloring book. Don't forget to
leave a review and share your finished pictures on Amazon.

ISBN 9798362459789

THIS BOOK BELONGS TO

ANKYLOSAURUS

AN-KIE-LOH-SORE-US
NAME MEANING: STIFF LIZARD

ONE OF THE LARGEST ARMOURED DINOSAURUS.
ANKYLOSAURUS HAD A WIDE, HEAVILY ARMOURED SKULL
AND A LARGE TAIL CLUB. IT HAD A LARGE GUT SPACE
FOR DIGESTING PLANT MATERIAL.

LENGTH: 7.0M   DIET: HERBIVOROUS

HEIGHT: 1.7M

WEIGHT: 4000KG   FOUND IN: CANADA, USA

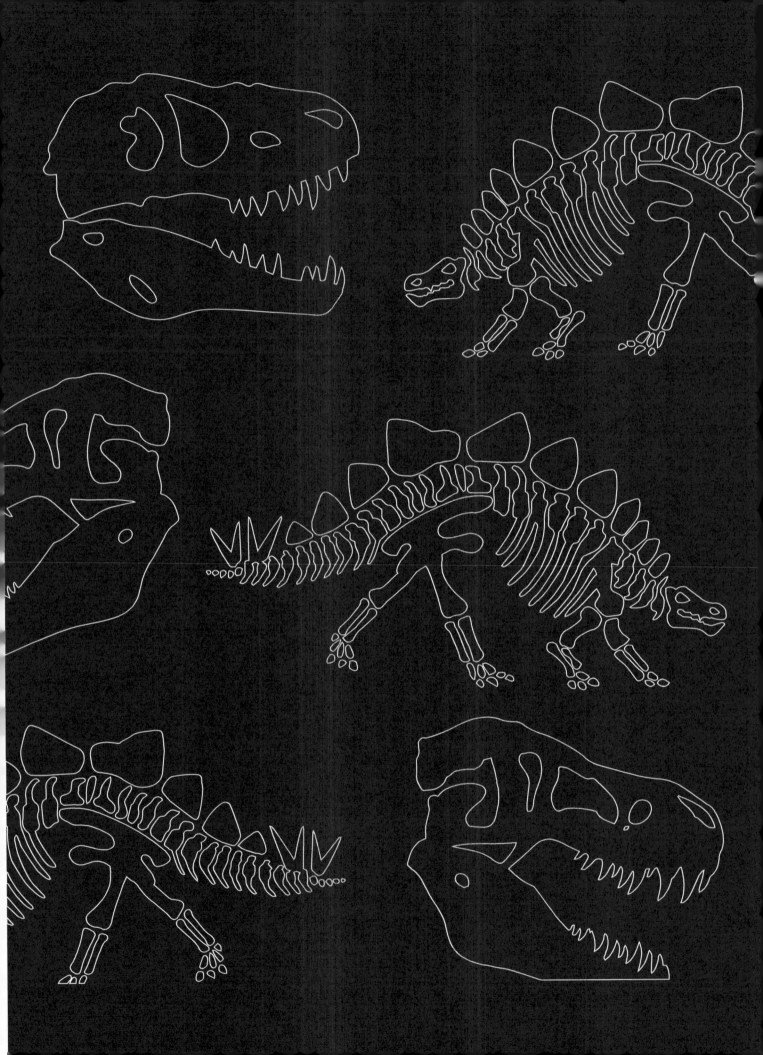

ALLOSAURUS

AL-OH-SAW-RUSS
NAME MEANING: OTHER LIZARD

THE TEETH OF ALLOSAURUS WERE 5-10CM LONG AND CURVED BACKWARDS TO PREVENT PREY FROM ESCAPING.

LENGTH: 12.0M
HEIGHT: 5.0M
WEIGHT: 2000KG

DIET: CARNIVOROUS
FOUND IN: PORTUGAL, USA

ARCHAEOPTERYX

ARK-EE-OPT-ER-IX
NAME MEANING: ANCIENT WING

ARCHAEOPTERYX HAD RAZOR SHARP TEETH, LONG BONY TAIL, AND COULD FLY

LENGTH: 0.5M
HEIGHT: 0.5M
WEIGHT: 1KG

DIET: CARNIVOROUS
FOUND IN: GERMANY

BRACHIOSAURUS

BRAK-EE-OH-SORE-US
NAME MEANING: ARM LIZARD

BRACHIOSAURUS HELD ITS HEAD VERY HIGH TO EAT THE LEAVES ON TALL TREE-LIKE PLANTS. THEY ATE BETWEEN 400 AND 900 POUNDS OF FOOD A DAY.

LENGTH: 30.0M
HEIGHT: 12M
WEIGHT: 25,400KG

DIET: HERBIVOROUS

FOUND IN: ALGERIA, PORTUGAL, TANZANIA, USA

CARNOTAURUS

KAR-NOH-TORE-US
NAME MEANING: CARNIVOROUS BULL

CARNOTAURUS HAD SHORTER ARMS THAN ANY OTHER
LARGE MEAT-EATING DINOSAURS. YES, ITS ARMS WERE
EVEN SHORTER THAN THE FAMOUSLY SHORT-ARMED T-REX!

LENGTH: 7.6M
HEIGHT: 3M
WEIGHT: 2,100KG

DIET: CARNIVOROUS

FOUND IN: ARGENTINA

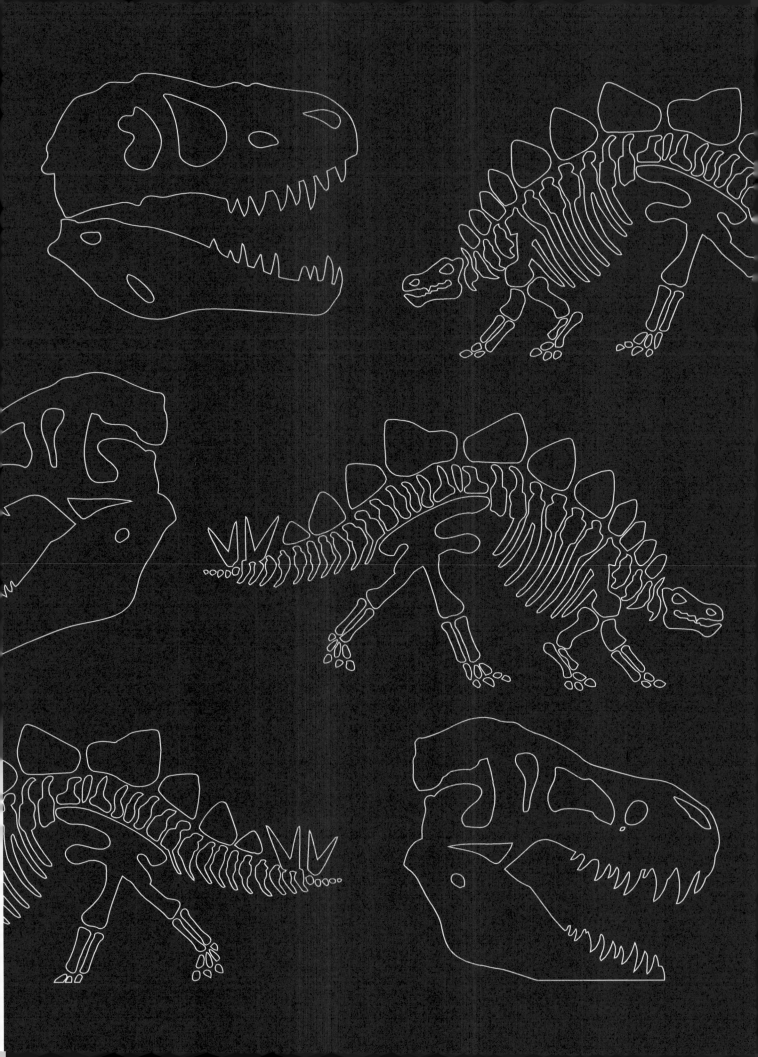

DIPLODOCUS

DIP-LOW DOCK-US
NAME MEANING: DOUBLE BEAM

ADULT DIPLODOCUSES WERE SO LARGE THAT EVEN THE MOST AGGRESSIVE PREDATORS WOULDN'T BRAVE AN ATTACK ON ONE.

LENGTH: 26.0M

HEIGHT: 4.6M

WEIGHT: 15000KG

DIET: HERBIVOROUS

FOUND IN: USA

ELAPHROSAURUS

EL-A-FRO-SORE-US
NAME MEANING: LIGHT-FOOTED LIZARD

ELAPHROSAURUS WAS A FAST, BIPEDAL (WALKED ON TWO LEGS), MEAT-EATING DINOSAUR. IT HAD SHORT, THIN ARMS WITH 3-FINGERED HANDS, STRONG, LONG-SHINNED LEGS, 3-TOED FEET, A LONG THIN NECK AND A STIFF TAIL.

LENGTH: 6.2M

HEIGHT: 1.5M

WEIGHT: 210KG

DIET: CARNIVOROUS

FOUND IN: TANZANIA

FUKUISAURUS

FOO-KOO-I-SORE-US
NAME MEANING: FUKUI LIZARD

FUKUISAURUS IS ONLY KNOWN FROM A SKULL, SO THE REST OF THE RECONSTRUCTION IS GUESSWORK BASED ON SIMILAR DINOSAURS.

LENGTH: 4.7M

HEIGHT: 4.5M

WEIGHT: 400KG

DIET: HERBIVOROUS

FOUND IN: JAPAN

GARUDIMIMUS

GA-ROO-DEE-MEEM-US
NAME MEANING: GARUDA MIMIC

GARUDIMIMUS HAD RELATIVELY SHORT LEGS AND HEAVY FEET. PREVIOUSLY IT WAS THOUGHT THAT GARUDIMIMUS HAD A HORN AT THE TOP OF THE SKULL. HOWEVER, RECENT STUDIES HAVE SHOWN THAT THIS "HORN" WAS SIMPLY A MISPLACED SKULL BONE

LENGTH: 4.7M
HEIGHT: 3.35M
WEIGHT: 98KG

DIET: OMNIVOROUS

FOUND IN: MONGOLIA

GALLIMIMUS

GAL-LEE-MEEM-US
NAME MEANING: CHICKEN MIMIC

ALSO KNOWN AS "OSTRICH DINOSAURS" FROM THE
ORNITHOMIMID FAMILY. THEY WERE QUICK AND COULD RUN
AT SPEEDS OF 50MPH.

LENGTH: 6M
HEIGHT: 2M
WEIGHT: 200KG

DIET: OMNIVOROUS

FOUND IN: MONGOLIA

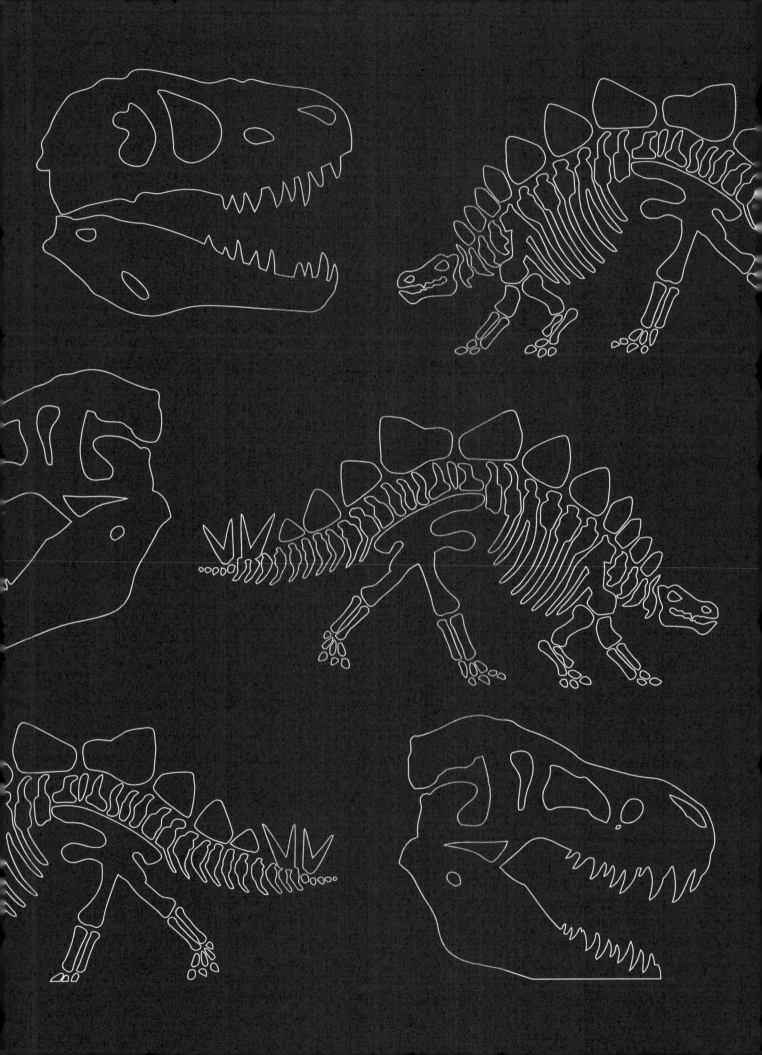

HYPSILOPHODON

HIP-SIH-LOH-FOH-DON
NAME MEANING: HIGH-RIDGE TOOTH

HYPSILOPHODON WAS A VERY FAST BI-PEDAL (TWO-LEGGED) RUNNER; ITS BACK LEGS WERE LONG. IT HAD A STIFFENED TAIL THAT HELPED IT BALANCE WHEN RUNNING.

LENGTH: 2.3M

HEIGHT: 0.6M

WEIGHT: 2KG

DIET: HERBIVOROUS

FOUND IN: ENGLAND, SPAIN, UNITED KINGDOM

IGUANODON

IG-WHA-NOH-DON
NAME MEANING: IGUANA TOOTH

IGUANODON COULD WALK ON ALL FOURS OR ON TWO LEGS.
IT HAD A LARGE THUMB SPIKE ON THE END OF ITS HAND
TO FEND-OFF PREDATORS.

LENGTH: 10M

HEIGHT: 2.7M

WEIGHT: 4000KG

DIET: HERBIVOROUS

FOUND IN: BELGIUM, ENGLAND,
UNITED KINGDOM

JURAVENATOR

JU-RAH-VE-NAY-TOR
NAME MEANING: JURA (BAVARIAN MOUNTAINS) HUNTER

JURAVENATOR IS AN EXTINCT GENUS OF SMALL-SIZED THEROPOD DINOSAURS. IT LIVED DURING THE JURASSIC ERA AND OCCUPIED THE FRANCONIAN JURA OF GERMANY

LENGTH: 0.8M

HEIGHT: 0.75M

WEIGHT: 0.5KG

DIET: CARNIVOROUS

FOUND IN: GERMANY

KRONOSAURUS

KRON-OH-SOR-US
NAME MEANING: LIZARD OF KRONOS

LIKE OTHER PLIOSAURS, KRONOSAURUS WAS A MARINE REPTILE.
IT HAD AN ELONGATED HEAD, A SHORT NECK, A STIFF BODY
PROPELLED BY FOUR FLIPPERS, AND A RELATIVELY SHORT TAIL.

LENGTH: 10M   **DIET: CARNIVOROUS**

WEIGHT: 12,100KG   **FOUND IN: AUSTRALIA**

ALEXORNIS

ALEX-ORN-NIS
NAME MEANING: ALEX'S ANCESTRAL BIRD

ALEXORNIS IS SIMILAR TO SOME MODERN BIRDS AND ONE OF THE FEW KNOWN CRETACEOUS "LAND BIRDS" MOST OTHER CRETACEOUS BIRDS AT THE TIME WERE THOUGHT TO BE AQUATIC OR SEMI-AQUATIC

LENGTH: 0.1M

WEIGHT: 0.1KG

DIET: HERBIVOROUS

FOUND IN: MEXICO

MOSASAURUS

MO-SAS-OR-US
NAME MEANING: LIZARD OF THE MEUSE RIVER

THE SKULL OF MOSASAURUS WAS EQUIPPED WITH ROBUST JAWS CAPABLE OF SWINGING BACK AND FORTH AND STRONG MUSCLES CAPABLE OF POWERFUL BITES USING DOZENS OF LARGE TEETH ADAPTED FOR CUTTING PREY.

LENGTH: 13M

WEIGHT: 14,000KG

DIET: CARNIVOROUS

FOUND IN: NETHERLANDS

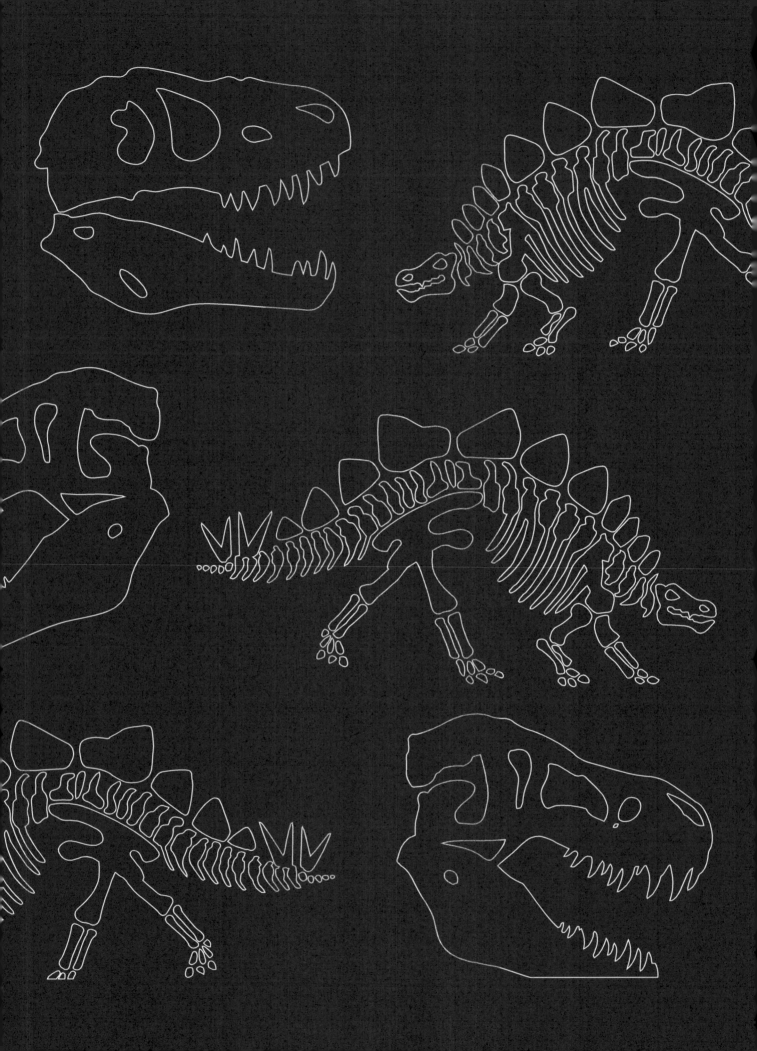

NOTHRONYCUS

NOH-THRON-I-KUS
NAME MEANING: SLOTHFUL CLAW

IT HAD LONG ARMS, A LONG NECK, A SMALL HEAD,
A TOOTHLESS BEAK, LEAF-SHAPED CHEEK TEETH,
AND A SHORT TAIL.

LENGTH: 5M
HEIGHT: 1.5M
WEIGHT: 1,000KG

DIET: OMNIVOROUS
FOUND IN: USA

OURANOSAURUS

OO-RAH-NOH-SORE-US
NAME MEANING: BRAVE MONITOR LIZARD

OURANOSAURUS HAS LONG THICK SPINES ON ITS BACK AND TAIL, SCIENTISTS BELIEVED THAT THESE SUPPORTED A LARGE FIN THAT WAS COVERED WITH SKIN.

LENGTH: 7.0M   DIET: HERBIVOROUS

WEIGHT: 4,000KG   FOUND IN: NIGER

PARASAUROLOPUS

PA-RA-SAW-ROL-OFF-US
NAME MEANING: BESIDE CRESTED LIZARD

THIS DINOSAUR HAD A LARGE CREST ON ITS HEAD USED FOR
TRUMPETING (PRODUCE LOUD SOUND). ON ADULT MALES THIS
CRESTCOULD BE AS LONG AS 1.8 METRES WHICH IS AS BIG
AS A MAN!

LENGTH: 11.0M   DIET: HERBIVOROUS
HEIGHT: 4.9M
WEIGHT: 3,500KG   FOUND IN: CANADA, USA

PTERODACTYL

TERR-UH-DAK-TUHL
NAME MEANING: WINGED FINGER

AS FAR AS SCIENTISTS KNOW, PTERODACTYLS WERE THE
LARGEST FLYING ANIMALS THAT EVER LIVED. SOME PTERODACTYLS
MEASURED MORE THAN 11 METERS ACROSS WITH THE WINGS
SPREAD OUT.

LENGTH: 11M   DIET: CARNIVOROUS
HEIGHT: 5.5M
WEIGHT: 250KG   FOUND IN: GERMANY

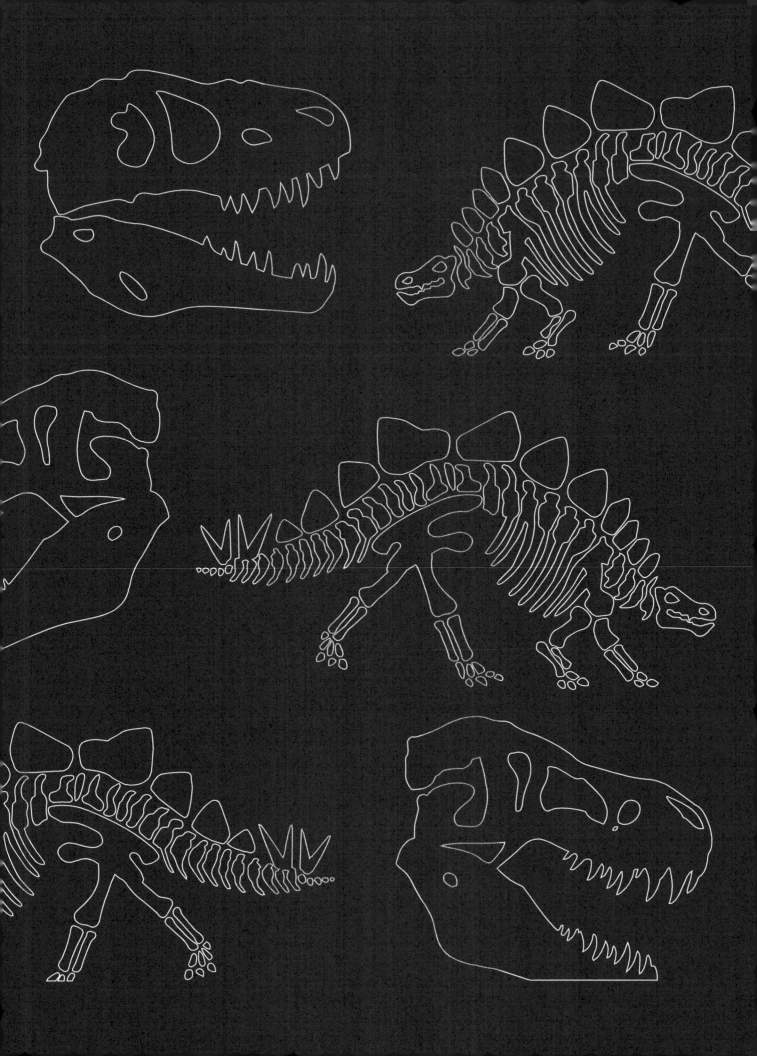

QUAESITOSAURUS

KWEE-SIET-OH-SORE-US
NAME MEANING: EXTRAORDINARY LIZARD

QUAESITOSAURUS WAS A HUGE, LONG-NECKED, WHIP-TAILED, PLANT-EATING DINOSAUR THAT WAS FOUND IN THE GOBI DESERT IN MONGOLIA AND LIVED ABOUT 80 MILLION YEARS AGO.

LENGTH: 23M
HEIGHT: 7.6M
WEIGHT: 6,350KG

DIET: HERBIVOROUS
FOUND IN: MONGOLIA

REBBACHISAURUS

RE-BASH-I-SORE-US
NAME MEANING: REBBACH LIZARD

LIKE OTHER MEMBERS OF ITS FAMILY, IT IS DISTINGUISHED
FROM OTHER SAUROPODS BY A TALL RIDGE DOWN ITS BACK.
IT HAD A LONG, GRACEFUL NECK AND A WHIP-LIKE TAIL.

LENGTH: 20M   DIET: HERBIVOROUS
HEIGHT: 14M
WEIGHT: 4,000KG   FOUND IN: AFRICA

STEGOSAURUS

STEG-OH-SORE-US
NAME MEANING: ROOF LIZARD

A LARGE, SLOW MOVING PLANT-EATER, STEGOSAURUS WOULD HAVE DEFENDED ITSELF FROM PREDATORS LIKE ALLOSAURUS AND CERATOSAURUS WITH ITS POWERFUL SPIKED TAIL.

LENGTH: 9M

HEIGHT: 4M

WEIGHT: 2,000KG

DIET: HERBIVOROUS

FOUND IN: USA

TYRANNOSAURUS

TIE-RAN-OH-SORE-US
NAME MEANING: TYRANT LIZARD KING

TYRANNOSAURUS LIVES UP TO ITS REPUTATION AS ONE OF THE MOST FEARSOME ANIMALS OF ALL TIME. ITS POWERFUL JAWS HAD 60 TEETH, EACH ONE UP TO 8 INCHES LONG AND ITS BITE WAS AROUND 3 TIMES AS POWERFUL THAN THAT OF A LION.

LENGTH: 12.0M
HEIGHT: 6M
WEIGHT: 7,000KG

DIET: CARNIVOROUS
FOUND IN: CANADA, USA

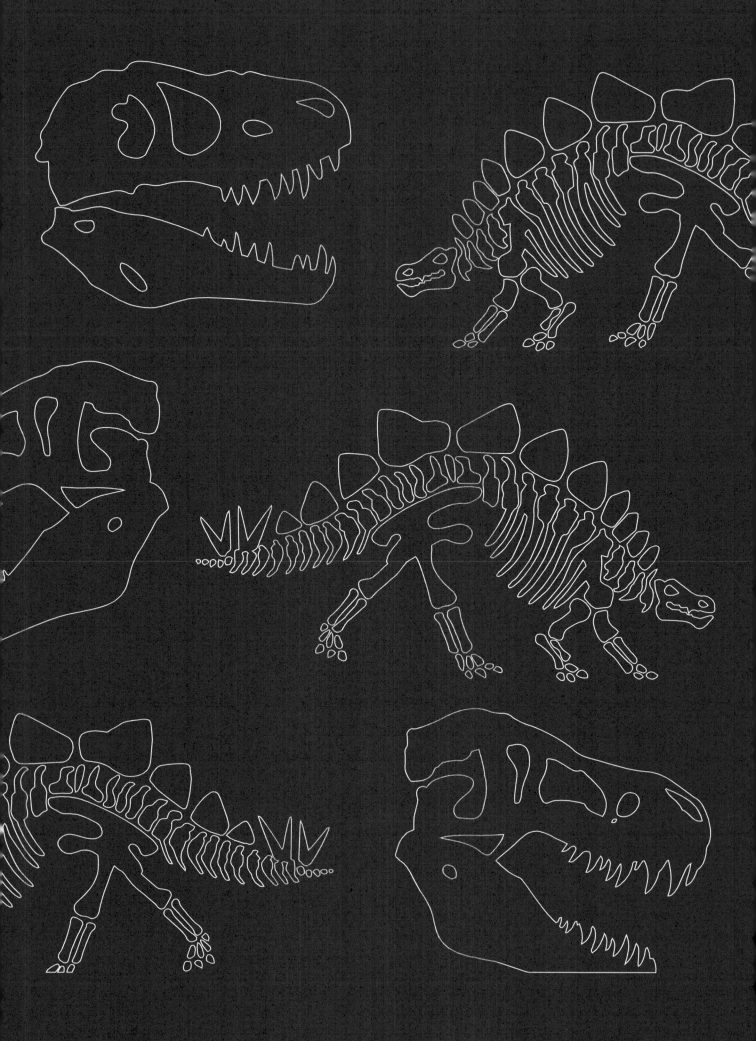

TRICERATOPS

TRI-SERRA-TOPS
NAME MEANING: THREE-HORNED FACE

WITH ITS 3 HORNS, A PARROT-LIKE BEAK AND A LARGE FRILL THAT COULD REACH NEARLY 1 METRE ACROSS, THE TRICERATOPS SKULL IS ONE OF THE LARGEST AND MOST STRIKING OF ANY LAND ANIMAL.

LENGTH: 9M
HEIGHT: 3M
WEIGHT: 5,500KG

DIET: HERBIVOROUS
FOUND IN: USA

URBACODON

URB-AH-KO-DON
NAME MEANING: URBAC TOOTH

THE URBACODON SIZE IS ASSUMED TO HAVE BEEN SMALL.
IT HAD A SET OF CLOSELY-PACKED TEETH. IT LIVED DURING
THE LATE CRETACEOUS PERIOD.

LENGTH: 1M
HEIGHT: 1.2M
WEIGHT: 10KG

DIET: CARNIVOROUS
FOUND IN: UZBEKISTAN

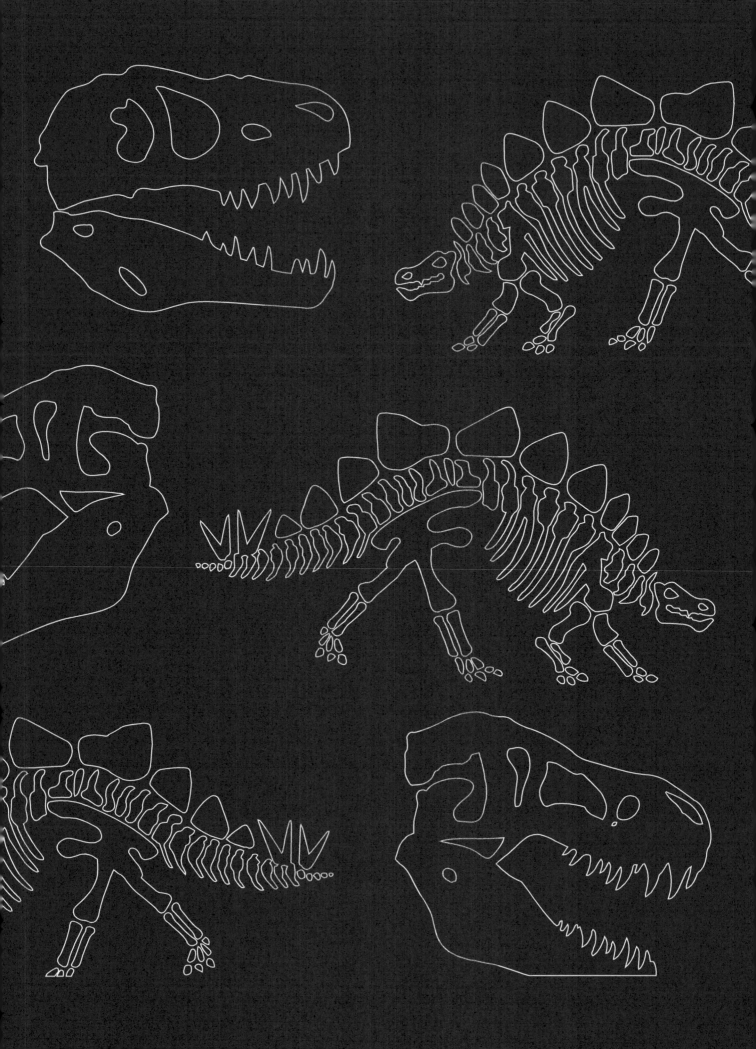

VELOCIRAPTOR

VEL-OSS-EE-RAP-TOR
NAME MEANING: QUICK PLUNDERER

VELOCIRATOR LIKELY HUNTED SOLO USING THEIR CLAWS TO
CLUTCH RATHER THAN SLASH PREY. THEY ROAMED CENTRAL
AND EASTERN ASIA BETWEEN ABOUT 74 MILLION AND 70 MILLION
YEARS AGO, DURING THE LATE CRETACEOUS PERIOD.

LENGTH: 1.8M
HEIGHT: 1.6M
WEIGHT: 45KG

DIET: CARNIVOROUS

FOUND IN: MONGOLIA

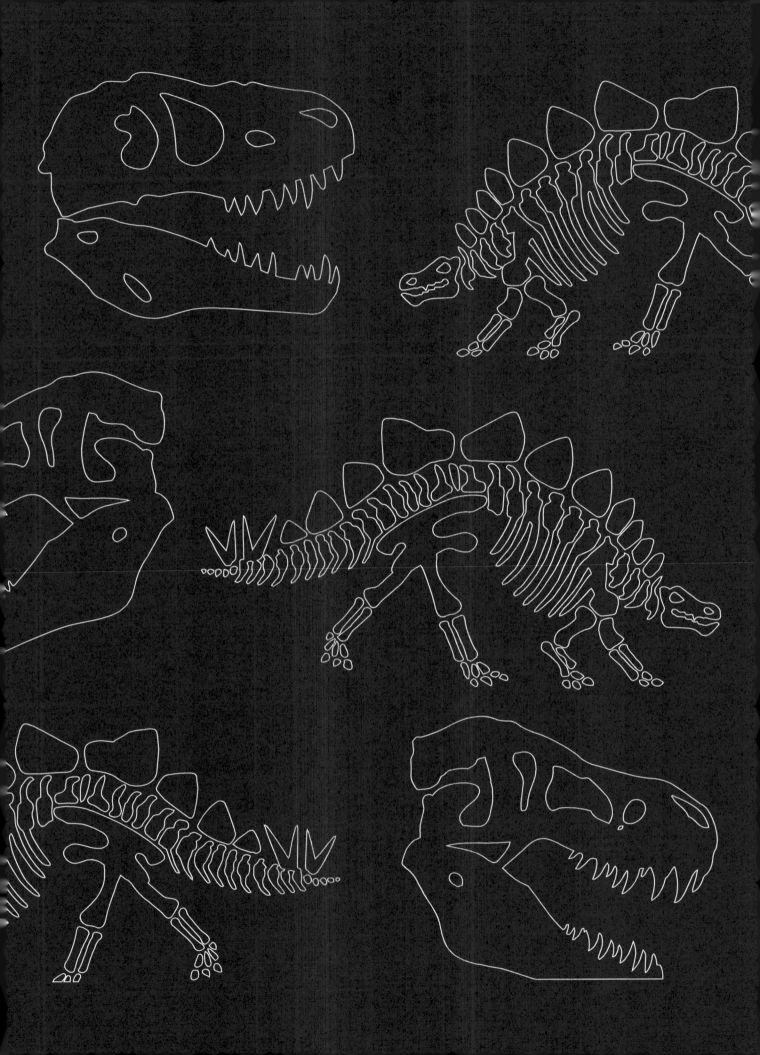

WUERHOSAURUS

WOO-EHR-HO-SAWR-US
NAME MEANING: LIZARD FROM WUERHO (CHINA)

IT HAD BONY, ROUNDED PLATES ALONG ITS BACK AND 4 BONY
SPIKES AT THE TIP OF ITS TAIL. IT WAS ONE OF THE LAST
GENERA OF STEGOSAUR KNOWN TO SURVIVE, SINCE MOST OTHERS
DIED OUT BY THE END OF THE JURASSIC

LENGTH: 7M
HEIGHT: 3M
WEIGHT: 4,400KG

DIET: CARNIVOROUS
FOUND IN: CHINA, MONGOLIA

XENOTARSOSAURUS

ZEE-NOH-TAR-SUH-SAW-RUS
NAME MEANING: STRANGE TARSUS LIZARD

XENOTARSOSAURUS IS A MEAT-EATING THEROPOD. IT LIVED DURING THE LATE CRETACEOUS PERIOD. IT HAD A LARGE BACKBONE WITH A KNOBBLY BACK. THERE ARE ALSO TWO HORNS ABOVE THE EYES. IT HAD SMALL ARMS, LIKE THE WELL KNOWN T-REX

LENGTH: 5.5M
HEIGHT: 6.7M
WEIGHT: 750KG

DIET: CARNIVOROUS
FOUND IN: ARGENTINA

YINLONG

YING-LONG
NAME MEANING: HIDDEN DRAGON

YINLONG WAS A RELATIVELY SMALL DINOSAUR. IT HAD LONG ROBUST HINDLIMBS AND SHORTER SLENDER FORELIMBS WITH THREE-FINGERED HANDS.

LENGTH: 1.2M

HEIGHT: 3.9M

WEIGHT: 15KG

DIET: HERBIVOROUS

FOUND IN: CHINA

ZEPHYROSAURUS

ZEF-EAR-RO-SORE-US
NAME MEANING: WEST WIND LIZARD

AMONG OTHER DISTINCTIVE CHARACTERISTICS, IT HAD A
STEEP FACE, A RAISED KNOB ON THE UPPER JAW, AND A LARGER
KNOB ON THE CHEEKBONE

LENGTH: 1.8M

HEIGHT: 1M

WEIGHT: 2,100KG

DIET: HERBIVOROUS

FOUND IN: USA

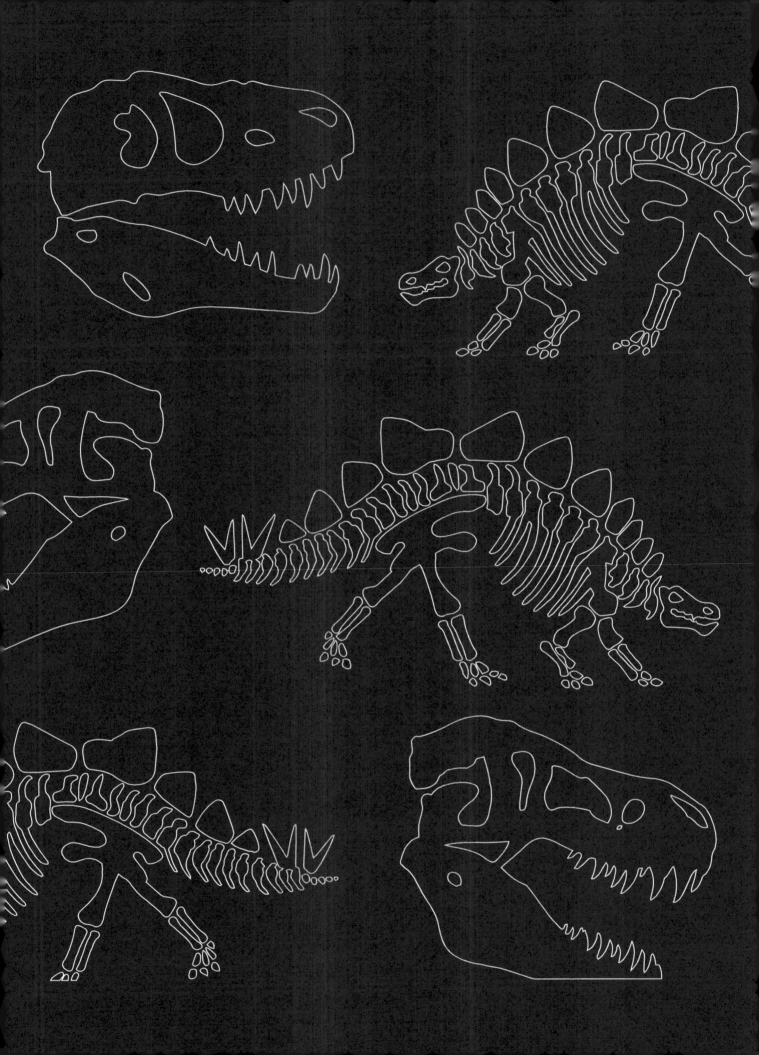

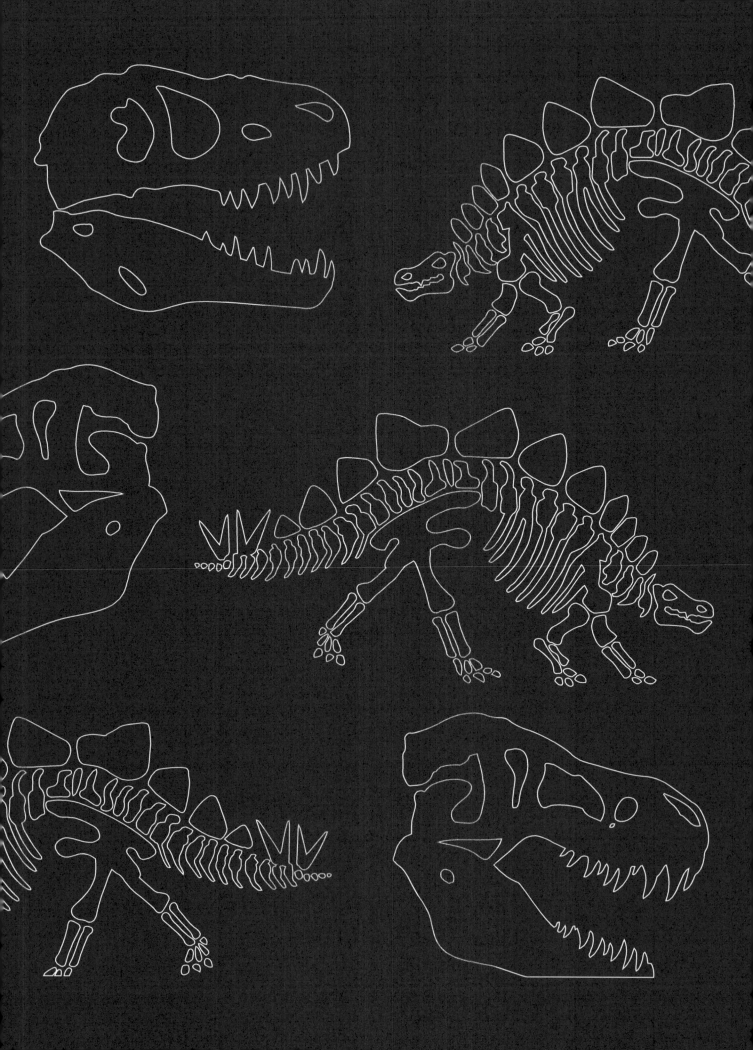

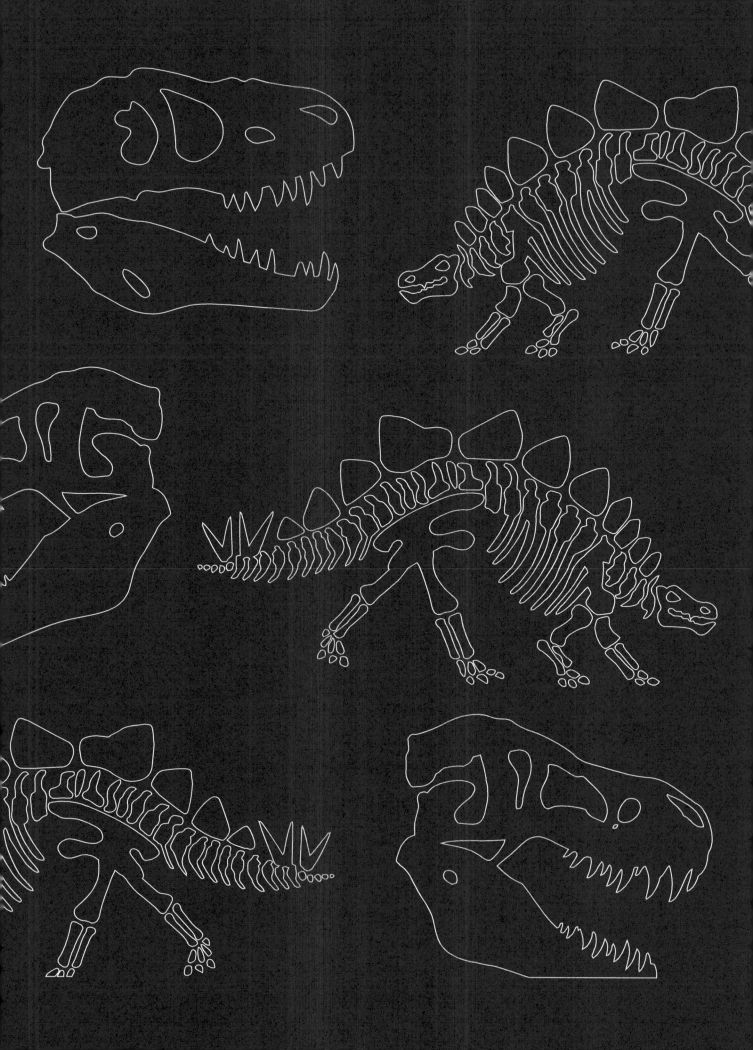

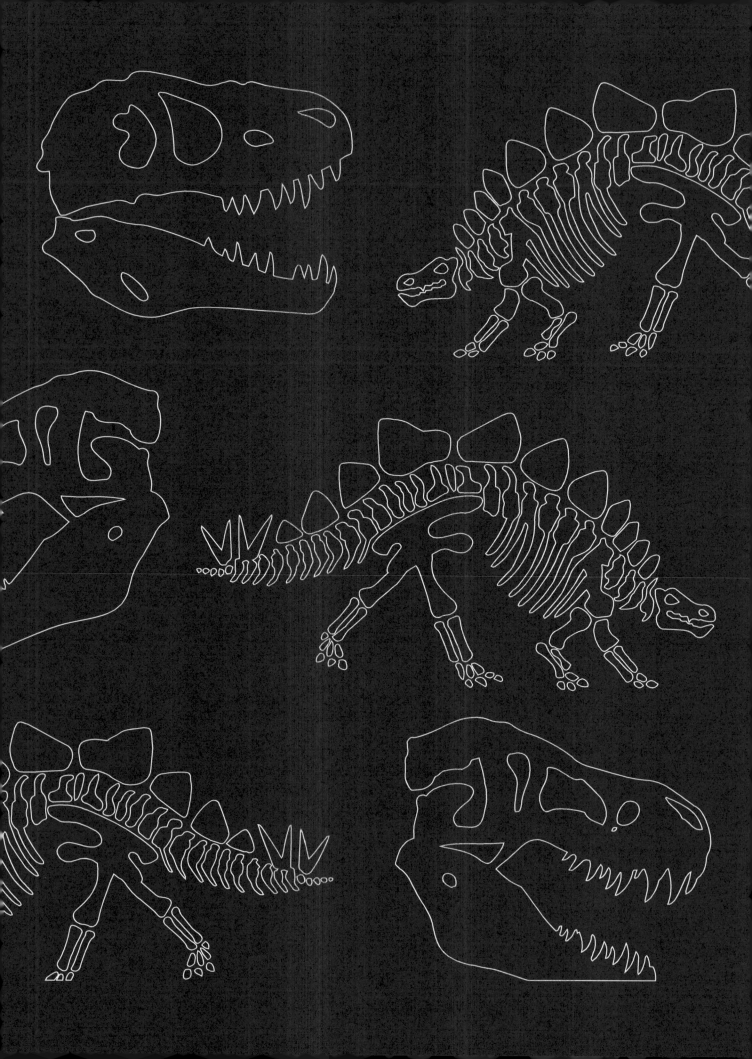

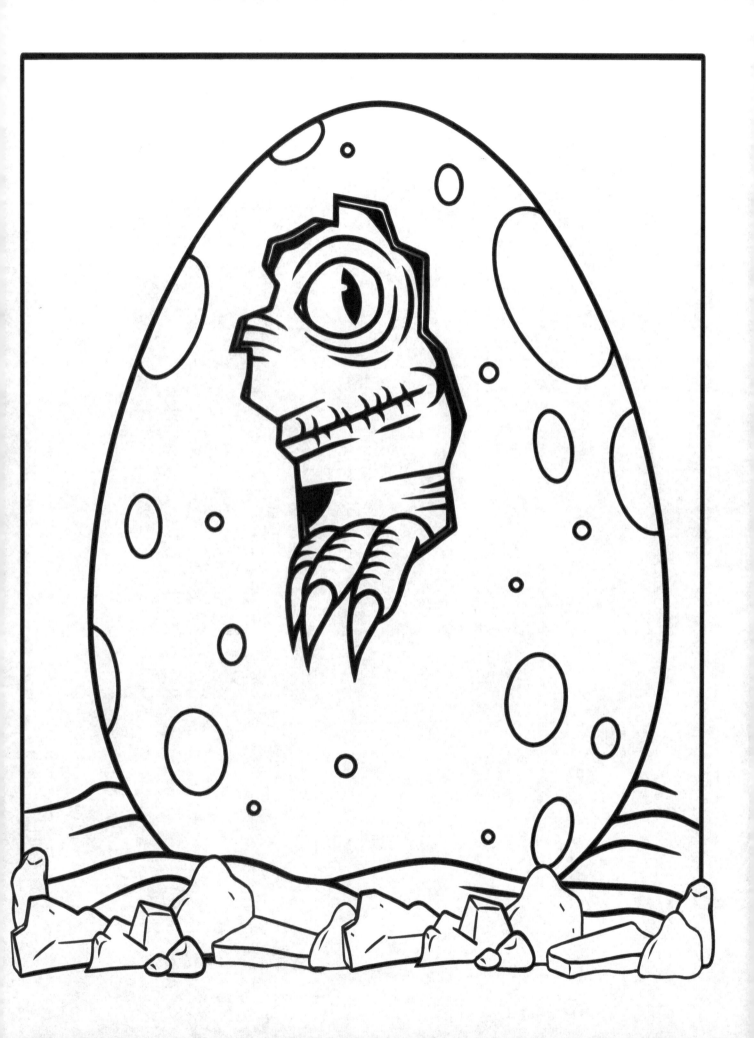

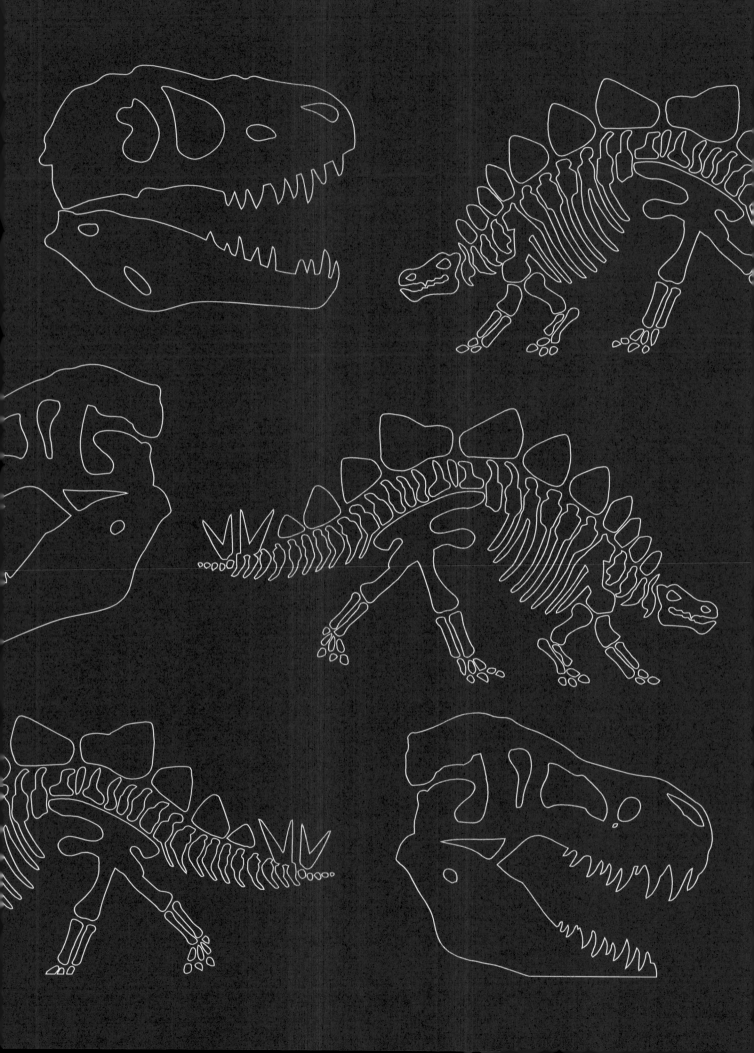

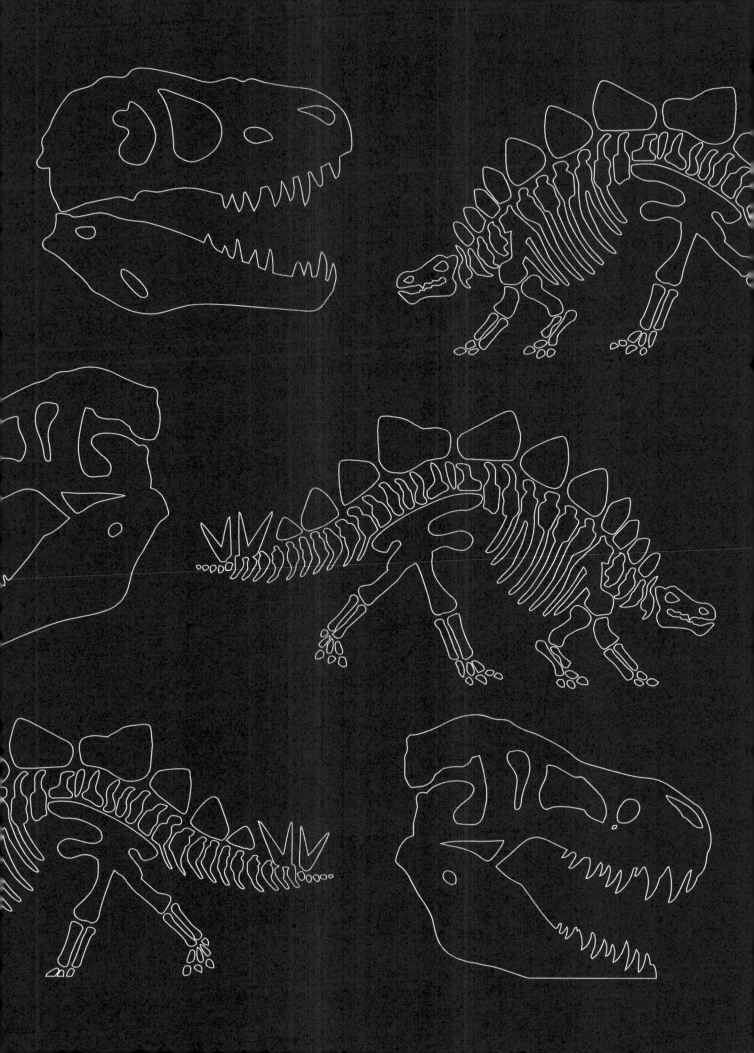

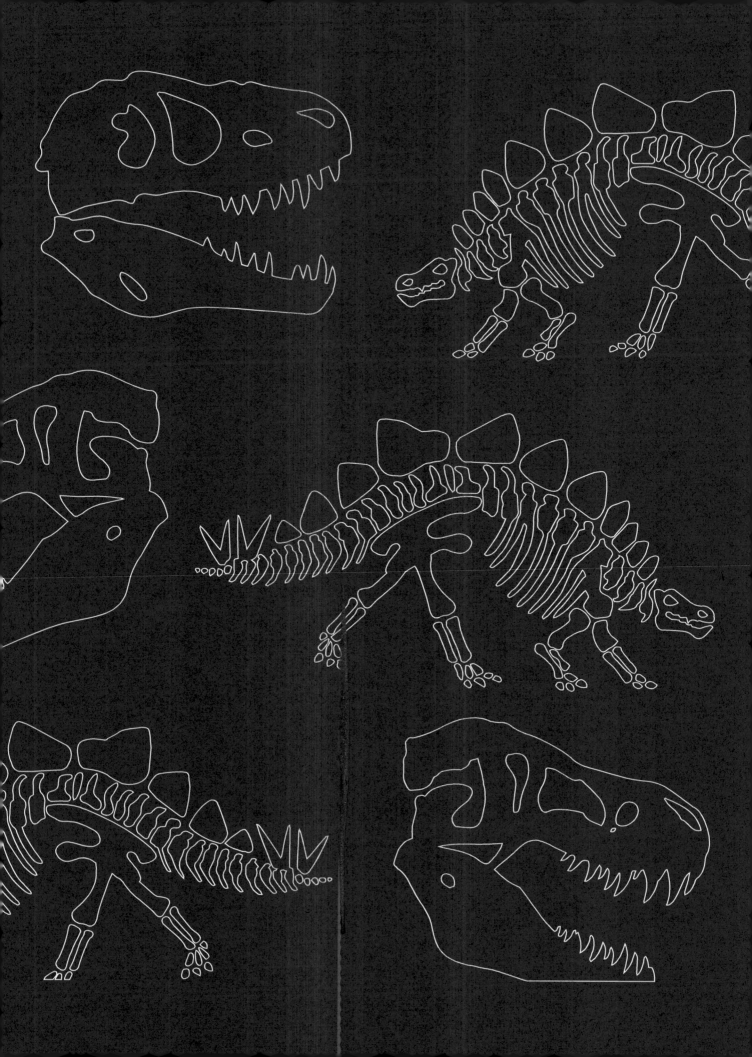

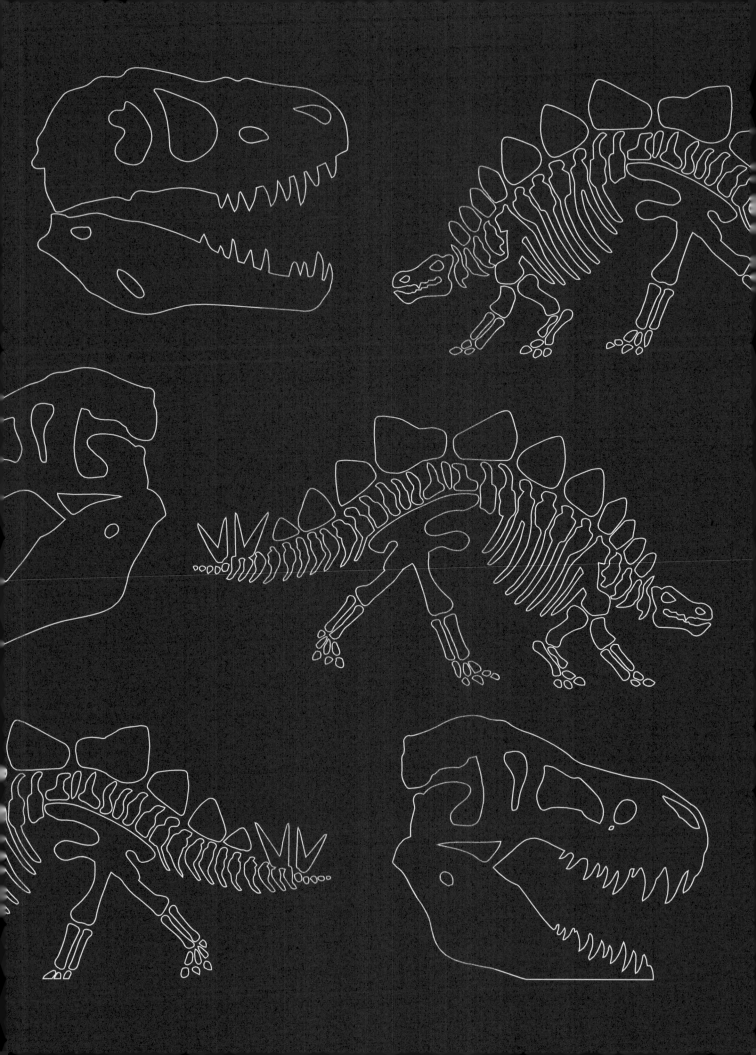

Long Neck Dinosaur

Brontosaurus

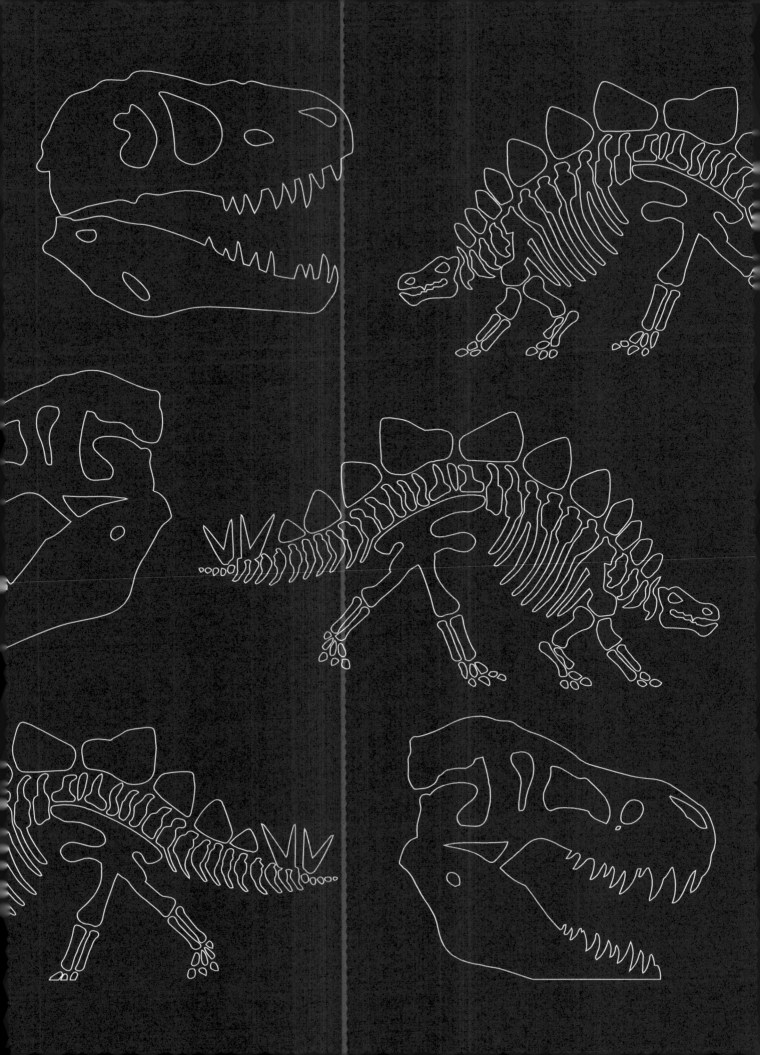

19097094R00060